Lerner SPORTS



GREATEST OF ALL TIME PLAYERS

# G.O.A.T. FOOTBALL KICKOFF AND PUNT RETURNERS

Audrey Stewart

Lerner Publications ◆ Minneapolis

Lerner Publications Company
An imprint of Lerner Publishing Group, Inc.
241 First Avenue North
Minneapolis, MN 55401 USA

For reading levels and more information, look up this title at www.lernerbooks.com.

Main body text set in Aptifer Sans LT Pro.
Typeface provided by Linotype AG.

**Library of Congress Cataloging-in-Publication Data**

Names: Stewart, Audrey, author.
Title: G.O.A.T. football kickoff and punt returners / Audrey Stewart.
Other titles: Greatest of all time football kick and punt returners
Description: Minneapolis, MN : Lerner Publications, [2025] | Series: Lerner sports. Greatest of all time players | Includes bibliographical references and index. | Audience: Ages 7–11 | Audience: Grades 2–3 | Summary: "Kick and punt returners create some of the most exciting plays in football. The greatest returners can win big games for their teams. Learn about the importance of returns and meet the game's best returners"—Provided by publisher.
Identifiers: LCCN 2023049827 (print) | LCCN 2023049828 (ebook) | ISBN 9798765625828 (library binding) | ISBN 9798765628782 (paperback) | ISBN 9798765633809 (epub)
Subjects: LCSH: Football players—United States—Biography—Juvenile literature. | Football players—Rating of—United States—Juvenile literature.
Classification: LCC GV939.A1 S747 2025 (print) | LCC GV939.A1 (ebook) | DDC 796.332092/2—dc23/eng/20231122

LC record available at https://lccn.loc.gov/2023049827
LC ebook record available at https://lccn.loc.gov/2023049828

Manufactured in the United States of America
1 – CG – 7/15/24

# TABLE OF CONTENTS

Dante Hall played wide receiver and returned kicks and punts for the Kansas City Chiefs. In seven seasons with the team, he logged 12,356 total return yards.

# SPEED AND SKILL

The Kansas City Chiefs were playing the Denver Broncos in October 2003. Both football teams were unbeaten for the season. The score was tied 7–7 early in the game. Broncos kicker Jason Elam made a 48-yard field goal to send the Broncos ahead 10–7. Then Chiefs kicker Morten Anderson tied the game 10–10. At the end of the second quarter, another field goal from Elam put the Broncos up 13–10.

# FACTS AT A GLANCE

- IN 2013, CORDARRELLE PATTERSON SET THE NATIONAL FOOTBALL LEAGUE (NFL) RECORD FOR LONGEST KICK RETURN AT 109 YARDS.
- DEVIN HESTER HOLDS THE NFL RECORD FOR MOST PUNTS RETURNED FOR A TOUCHDOWN WITH 14.
- DANTE HALL SET A RECORD FOR THE KANSAS CITY CHIEFS WITH 12,356 TOTAL RETURN YARDS.
- JOSHUA CRIBBS IS ONE OF ONLY TWO NFL PLAYERS TO HAVE TWO KICKOFF RETURN TOUCHDOWNS OF 100 YARDS OR MORE IN A SINGLE GAME.

Both teams wanted to hold on to their win streaks. In the fourth quarter, the Broncos kicked another field goal to go ahead 23–17. With eight minutes left, Chiefs returner Dante Hall caught the kickoff. He dodged Broncos defenders and ran a wide loop across the field. Once he was in the clear, he sprinted down the field for a 93-yard touchdown.

Dante Hall

The Broncos could not score again, and the Chiefs won 24–23. Kansas City finished the regular season first in the American Football Conference (AFC) with a 13–3 record. Dante Hall tied an NFL record that season with four straight games with a kickoff or punt return for a touchdown.

A returner's job is to catch kickoffs and punts and run the ball back up the field. Returns can also happen if a kicker misses a field goal. If the kick is short, defenders can catch the ball and try to run it back. Returners are some of the fastest runners on the team. They use skills such as spin moves and quick feet to carry the ball as far as possible.

In his first NFL season, returner and wide receiver Devin Hester led the league in return touchdowns.

Joshua Cribbs was a successful quarterback in college, but he made NFL history as a kick and punt returner for the Cleveland Browns.

They usually play other positions too, such as wide receiver or running back.

A punt is kicked from anywhere on the field. Teams usually punt on fourth down when they are too far away to kick a field goal. A kickoff happens from the same spot for each team. In the NFL, teams kick off from the 35-yard line. Kickoffs take place at the start of each half and after scores.

Kick and punt returners can make a huge difference for their teams. Speedy returners gain big yards and make it easier to score. The NFL's best returners score touchdowns and can be the difference between winning and losing.

# NO. 10 TYREEK HILL

Tyreek Hill is fast. During one NFL game, he sprinted down the field during a return and had time to high-five a teammate before running into the end zone. The Kansas City Chiefs picked Hill in the fifth round of the 2016 NFL Draft. He began the 2016 season as Kansas City's starting punt and kick returner. He was also a wide receiver.

That season, Hill was the AFC Offensive Player of the Week after a 30–27 victory over the Denver Broncos in week 12. He returned a kick 86 yards to score a touchdown to help beat Denver. The Chiefs went 12–4 that season. In 2018, Hill's first touch of the ball was a 91-yard punt return for a touchdown against the Los Angeles Chargers. The Chiefs started the season with a 38–28 win.

In 2020, Hill and the Chiefs won the Super Bowl. They made a second Super Bowl appearance in 2021, but the Chiefs lost to the Tampa Bay Buccaneers. Hill is an eight-time Pro Bowl player and was a First-Team All-Pro player in 2016, 2018, 2020, and 2022.

## TYREEK HILL STATS

| | |
|---|---|
| Punt-Return Touchdowns | 4 |
| Kickoff-Return Touchdowns | 1 |
| Longest Punt Return | 95 Yards |
| Longest Kickoff Return | 86 Yards |

Stats are accurate through the 2023 NFL season.

# NO. 9 ERIC METCALF

Eric Metcalf did a lot in only six years as an NFL player. He played for the Cleveland Browns as a returner, wide receiver, and running back. The Browns picked Metcalf in the first-round of the 1989 NFL Draft. In his second season, he led the NFL with 1,052 kickoff return yards and two return touchdowns. Metcalf also led the NFL in punt return touchdowns in 1993, 1994, and 1995.

In 1997, Metcalf played one season as a receiver with the San Diego Chargers. Metcalf was a kick returner for the Pro Bowl that year. He is a three-time Pro Bowl player and a two-time First-Team All-Pro. Metcalf finished his NFL career with the Green Bay Packers in 2002. He had 541 career catches and is fifth in NFL history with 3,453 punt return yards. Metcalf's 12 career return touchdowns are tied for sixth in the NFL.

## ERIC METCALF STATS

| | |
|---|---|
| Punt-Return Touchdowns | 10 |
| Kickoff-Return Touchdowns | 2 |
| Punt-Return Yards | 3,453 |
| Kickoff-Return Yards | 5,813 |

NO. 8

# DANTE HALL

The NFL Network ranked Dante Hall the 10th best returner in NFL history. His career began when the Kansas City Chiefs picked Hall in the 2000 NFL Draft. In 2002, he had two punt-return touchdowns. That season, Hall played in his first Pro Bowl as a returner.

Hall holds many Chiefs return records. In 2003, he had a return touchdown in four straight games. This was Hall's best season. He was a First-Team All-Pro and played in the Pro Bowl that year. Nine of Hall's 12 career touchdowns happened between 2002 and 2004.

In 2006, one of his last NFL seasons, Hall returned two kickoffs in a game. With these returns, he became the sixth player in NFL history to have 10,000 career kick return yards. Hall finished his career with 12,397 total return yards.

## DANTE HALL STATS

| | |
|---|---|
| Punt-Returns | 216 |
| Punt-Return Touchdowns | 6 |
| Kickoff Returns | 426 |
| Kickoff-Return Touchdowns | 6 |

# NO. 7 ALLEN ROSSUM

Allen Rossum is the Atlanta Falcons' all-time leader in punt returns with 1,723 yards and kickoff returns with 5,489 yards gained over five seasons. He started out with the Philadelphia Eagles after the 1998 NFL Draft. In 2002, he became a returner and pass defender for the Falcons.

The 2003 season was his best on record. Rossum played in all 16 games and led the NFL in punt return yards with 545. The following season, the Falcons went 11–5, and Rossum played in the Pro Bowl.

In 2005, Rossum made NFL history for gaining the most punt return yards in a playoff game. He earned 152 yards on three returns. Rossum's first return of that game was a touchdown that gave the Falcons a 28–14 lead. Although the Falcons lost the next game, Rossum had 1,432 kick return yards and 629 punt return yards for the season and the playoffs.

## ALLEN ROSSUM STATS

| | |
|---|---|
| Punt Returns | 307 |
| Punt-Return Touchdowns | 3 |
| Kickoff-Return Touchdowns | 5 |
| Longest Kickoff Return | 104 Yards |

## NO. 6 BRIAN MITCHELL

Brian Mitchell is one of the greatest Washington Commanders players of all time. He spent 14 seasons in the NFL. Ten of those were with Washington as a returner and running back. Mitchell holds three different NFL records. He has the most kickoff return yards with 14,014, the most punt return yards with 4,999, and the most combined return yards with 19,013.

Mitchell's first NFL play was in a preseason game. He returned the opening kickoff for a touchdown. In his second NFL season, Mitchell led the NFL in punt return yards and punts returned for a touchdown. His skills as a return specialist helped Washington make it to the Super Bowl in 1992. They beat the Buffalo Bills 37–24.

Later in his career, Mitchell was both a top kickoff returner and a top punt returner. In 2002, he returned a punt 76 yards for his 13th career return touchdown. The play broke the previous NFL record for most kick and punt returns for touchdowns.

## BRIAN MITCHELL STATS

| | |
|---|---|
| Punt Returns | 463 |
| Punt-Return Yards | 4,999 |
| Longest Punt Return | 84 Yards |
| Kickoff and Punt-Return Touchdowns | 13 |

# NO. 5 CORDARRELLE PATTERSON

The Minnesota Vikings picked Cordarrelle Patterson in the first round of the 2013 NFL Draft. The talented athlete is a running back, wide receiver, and returner. Sometimes he even plays defense. Patterson tied the NFL record for the longest play ever in his rookie season. He caught a kickoff near the back of the end zone. Then he ran the ball 109 yards for a touchdown.

Patterson was most successful as a kick returner during his early career. In 2016, he played in his second Pro Bowl game. He recorded 52 catches, 25 kickoff returns, and one return touchdown that season.

While playing for the New England Patriots, Patterson helped the team win the 2019 Super Bowl. He was an NFL kickoff return yards leader in 2019 and 2020. During those seasons, he played in his third and fourth Pro Bowl games. Patterson is a four-time First-Team All-Pro. He holds the NFL record for most kickoff return touchdowns with nine.

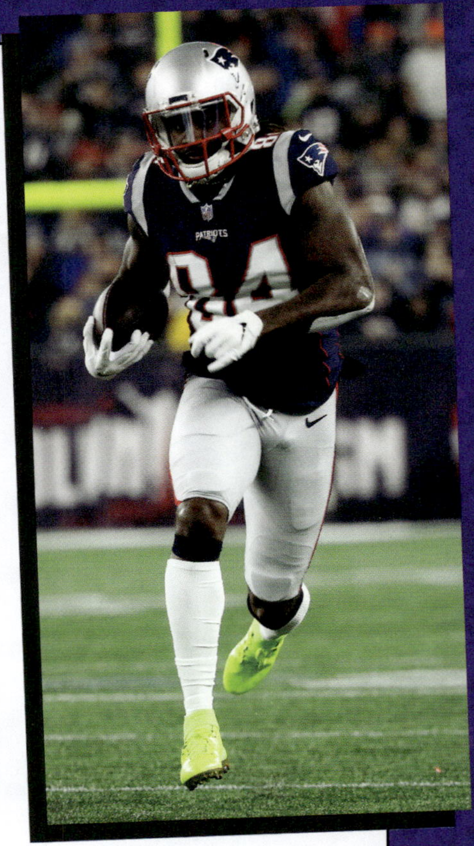


## CORDARRELLE PATTERSON STATS

| | |
|---|---|
| Kickoff Returns | 273 |
| Kickoff-Return Touchdowns | 9 |
| Kickoff-Return Yards | 7,989 |
| Longest Kickoff Return | 109 Yards |

Stats are accurate through the 2023 NFL season.

## NO. 4 GALE SAYERS

The Chicago Bears chose Gale Sayers fourth overall in the 1965 NFL Draft. He spent seven seasons with the Bears from 1965 to 1971. He scored 22 total touchdowns in his first season, setting an NFL record for most touchdowns by a rookie. He won the 1965 Rookie of the Year award.

What made Sayers unique was his ability to move around opponents. He played as a running back and a returner. He found holes in the defense and ran through them. Sayers could change direction and sprint past defenders with speed and skill. Before the defense could tackle him, Sayers was already halfway down the field.

A knee injury shortened his NFL career. Even though he only played for five full seasons, Sayers was still great enough to make the Pro Football Hall of Fame at the age of 34. He had 91 career kick returns and six kick-return touchdowns. He finished his career with 3,172 total return yards and eight return touchdowns.

## GALE SAYERS STATS

| | |
|---|---|
| Punt-Return Touchdowns | 2 |
| Kickoff-Return Touchdowns | 6 |
| Kickoff-Return Yards | 2,781 |
| Longest Punt Return | 85 Yards |

# NO. 3 RICK UPCHURCH

Rick Upchurch played wide receiver and returned kicks with the Denver Broncos from 1975 to 1983. He recorded 1,929 return yards in his first year with the team. In his second season, Upchurch set an NFL record with four punts returned for touchdowns. He also played in his first Pro Bowl game that season.

Upchurch helped the Broncos win 12 of 14 games in 1977. He led the league in punt return yards with 653, and the Broncos made it to their first Super Bowl. During the 1978

Super Bowl, the Broncos were losing 13–0 at halftime. The Broncos kicked a field goal for three points, but the Dallas Cowboys scored a touchdown to go ahead 20–3 in the third quarter. On the next kickoff, Upchurch caught the ball and zigzagged up the field for 67 yards. The Broncos scored to bring the score to 23–10. They lost the game, but Upchurch set a Super Bowl record for most return yards on a kickoff.

Upchurch had 24 career receiving touchdowns and 5,714 return yards. He played in four Pro Bowl games. After he retired from playing, Upchurch coached football at Tabor College in Kansas.

## RICK UPCHURCH STATS

| | |
|---|---|
| Punt Returns | 248 |
| Punt-Return Touchdowns | 8 |
| Longest Punt Return | 92 Yards |
| Longest Kickoff Return | 64 Yards |

# NO. 2 JOSHUA CRIBBS

Joshua Cribbs had a big impact on the Cleveland Browns in 2005. He joined the team as a kick returner and averaged 24.3 yards per return. Cribbs returned a kick 90 yards for a touchdown in a game against the Detroit Lions. In the 2007 season, he played in his first Pro Bowl.

For the 2007 season, Cribbs had a career high of 1,809 kickoff return yards. He averaged 30.7 yards per kickoff return. Cribbs set an NFL record with eight career kickoff returns for touchdowns.

In 2009, he tied an NFL record by returning two kickoffs at least 100 yards for touchdowns in a single game. He ran 100 yards in the first quarter and 103 yards in the second quarter in a game against the Chiefs. Cribbs played his final NFL game in 2014. He is ranked second in the NFL for career kickoff-return touchdowns.

## JOSHUA CRIBBS STATS

| | |
|---|---|
| Kickoff-Return Touchdowns | 8 |
| Kickoff-Return Yards | 11,113 |
| Punt-Return Touchdowns | 3 |
| Punt-Return Yards | 2,375 |

NO. 1

## DEVIN HESTER

Chicago Bears fans nicknamed Devin Hester the Windy City Flyer for his speed on the field. He joined the Bears for the 2006 season as a wide receiver and returner. As a rookie, Hester recorded six return touchdowns. He was part of the 2006 NFL All-Rookie Team.

In 2006, the Bears had a close win over the Arizona Cardinals. Hester played a key role. In the fourth quarter, he returned a punt 83 yards for a touchdown. The Bears won 24–23.

Hester played in the Pro Bowl in 2006, 2007, 2010, and 2014. He was the NFL Player of the Week 19 times. He holds the NFL record for most punts returned for touchdowns at 14.

Hester is the only player to return a Super Bowl kickoff for a touchdown. The Bears were playing the Indianapolis Colts in the 2007 Super Bowl. Hester returned the opening kickoff 92 yards for a touchdown and gave the Bears an early 7–0 lead.

## DEVIN HESTER STATS

| | |
| --- | --- |
| Punt Returns | 315 |
| Punt-Return Touchdowns | 14 |
| Kickoff Returns | 295 |
| Longest Kickoff Return | 98 Yards |

# EVEN MORE G.O.A.T.

There have been so many amazing kickoff and punt returners in NFL history. Choosing only 10 is a challenge. Here are 10 others who could have made the G.O.A.T. list.

| | |
|---|---|
| No. 11 | TERRENCE MCGEE |
| No. 12 | TIM BROWN |
| No. 13 | HERSCHEL WALKER |
| No. 14 | OLLIE MATSON |
| No. 15 | ABE WOODSON |
| No. 16 | MEL GRAY |
| No. 17 | DESMOND HOWARD |
| No. 18 | DESEAN JACKSON |
| No. 19 | TRAVIS WILLIAMS |
| No. 20 | MICHAEL LEWIS |

# YOUR G.O.A.T.

It's your turn to make a G.O.A.T. list about kickoff and punt returners. Start by doing research. Consider the rankings in this book. Then check out the Learn More section on page 31. Explore the books and websites to learn more about football players of the past and present.

You can search online for more information about great players too. Check with a librarian, who may have other resources for you. You might even try reaching out to football teams or players to see what they think.

Once you're ready, make your list of the greatest players of all time. Then ask people you know to make G.O.A.T. lists and compare them. Do you have players no one else listed? Are you missing anybody your friends think is important? Talk it over and try to convince them that your list is the G.O.A.T.!

# GLOSSARY

**draft:** when teams take turns choosing new players

**end zone:** the area at each end of a football field where players score touchdowns

**field goal:** a score of three points in football made by kicking the ball over the crossbar

**First-Team All-Pro:** a team made up of each season's best NFL players

**kickoff:** a kick that puts the ball into play to start each half or after a score

**punt:** when a football player drops the ball and kicks it before it touches the ground

**Pro Bowl:** the NFL's all-star game

**returner:** a player who returns kickoffs and punts

**return:** when a football player catches a kicked ball and carries it forward to gain yards

**rookie:** a first-year player

# LEARN MORE


Cooper, Robert. *Great Moments in NFL History*. Minneapolis: Discover Roo, 2020.

Football
https://kids.britannica.com/kids/article/football/353142

Football Kick Returns and Returning
https://www.rookieroad.com/football/101/kick-returns-and-returning/

Football Punt Returner
https://www.rookieroad.com/football/positions/punt-returner/

Levit, Joe. *G.O.A.T. Football Teams*. Minneapolis: Lerner Publications, 2021.

Scheff, Matt. *The Super Bowl: Football's Game of the Year*. Minneapolis: Lerner Publications, 2021.

# INDEX



# PHOTO ACKNOWLEDGMENTS

Image credits: Hyoung Chang/Contributor/Getty Images, p.4; The Sporting News/Contributor/Getty Images, p.5; Scott Cunningham/Contributor/Getty Images, p.6; Diamond Images/Contributor/Getty Images, p.7; Peter G. Aiken/Contributor/Getty Images, p.8; Brandon Sloter/Contributor/Getty Images, p.9; George Gojkovich/Contributor/Getty Images, p.10; Rick Stewart/Stringer/Getty Images, p.11; Peter Brouillet/Contributor/Getty Images, p.12; Sporting News Archive/Contributor/Getty Images, p.13; Craig Jones/Stringer/Getty Images, p.14; Ronald Martinez/Staff/Getty Images, p.15; Stringer/Getty Images, p.16; Mitchell Layton/Contributor/Getty Images, p.17; Lachlan Cunningham/Contributor/Getty Images, p.18; Adam Glanzman/Stringer/Getty Images, p.19; Focus On Sport/Contributor/Getty Images, p.20; Focus On Sport/Contributor/Getty Images, p.21; Clifton Boutelle/Contributor/Getty Images, p.22; Bettmann/Contributor/Getty Images, p.23; David Maxwell/Stringer/Getty Images, p.24; Andy Lyons/Staff/Getty Images, p.25; Jonathan Daniel/Staff/Getty Images, p.26; Diamond Images/Contributor/Getty Images, p.27

Cover: Tom Szczerbowski/Stringer/Getty Images; Grant Halverson/Contributor/Getty Images; Sam Greenwood/Staff/Getty Images